CW00482304

STUMPED AGAIN!

*More of the world's
funniest cricket quotes*

Crombie Jardine
Publishing Limited
Office 2
3 Edgar Buildings
George Street
Bath
BA1 2FJ
www.crombiejardine.com

ISBN: 978-1-906051-43-3

Copyright © Crombie Jardine Publishing Limited, 2010

Compiled by Crombie Jardine, 2010

All rights are reserved. No part of this publication may be
reproduced, stored in a retrieval system, or transmitted, in
any form or by any means, electronic, mechanical,
photocopying, recording or otherwise, without the prior
written permission of the publisher.

Printed and bound in China

Contents

Introduction

In our first compilation of cricket quotes and gaffes (STUMPED! THE WORLD'S FUNNIEST CRICKET QUOTES), we paid homage to cricket radio announcers. Whilst most sports commentators have an hour or so to fill, our cricket announcers have up to eight hours to spend keeping us informed and entertained. It's no wonder that they come out with the occasional howler or downright gaffe.

Some of Brian Johnston's gaffes are perhaps the most well-known ones. Who doesn't remember or hasn't heard of the Headingley Test in 1961, when Neil Harvey was representing Australia: "There's Neil Harvey standing at leg slip with his legs wide apart, waiting for a tickle." Not to mention the oft-cited quote, "The bowler's Holding, the batsman's Willey", allegedly uttered when Michael Holding of the West Indies was bowling to Peter Willey of England in a Test match at the Oval in 1976.

We make mention of these two famous quotes here because as a rule we haven't duplicated quotes from the first book but some just deserve a second mention! There is plenty of humour from the likes of Shane Warne ("I used to put on weight easily. I remember my dad picked me up at the airport and thought I was a fat bastard he didn't know") and Andrew Flintoff (on accepting a man of the match award, "Not bad for a fat lad") to fill the gap!

Like STUMPED! THE WORLD'S FUNNIEST CRICKET QUOTES, this book is dedicated to cricket people the world over. It's a sport that doesn't take itself too seriously and it's all the better for that.

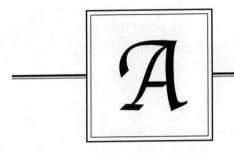

"A very small crowd here today.
I can count the people on one hand.
Can't be more than 30"
Michael Abrahamson, SABC

"Owais Shah is about to start
coming hard"
Chris Adams, Sky Sports

"Paul Collingwood is proving to be
a very good tosser"
Jonathan Agnew

"The more you force it, the less likely
it is to work"
Jonathan Agnew

"He didn't quite get his leg over"
*Jonathan Agnew, after Ian Botham had spun
around off balance and tried (unsuccessfully)
to step over the wicket*

"On the outfield, hundreds of small boys
are playing with their balls"
Rex Alston, BBC

"At least I don't wear mascara like
Alastair Cook"
Jimmy Anderson

"If they stop throwing, cricket
in Australia will die"
Tommy Andrews

"Kevin Pietersen's sticky patch
was a very small one"
Mike Atherton

"It is time for Indian cricket supporters
to grow up and accept defeat as an
essential part of the game. Sport is
not about winning; it is about losing.
Trust me, we in English cricket know
more about that than anyone"
*Mike Atherton, on the reaction of
Indian fans after India's exit from
the 2009 Twenty20 World Cup*

On the Mike Atherton ball-tampering row
"Athers to Athers, dust to dust"
Sign outside a pub in Reading, Berkshire (1994)

"Somerset's rent-a-quote, Peter Anderson, enjoyed another opportunity to stick the boot in, accusing the would-be reformers of knowing nothing about the game. It is undeniable, of course, that an ex-copper from Hong Kong should know more about cricket than the combined experience of two England captains"
Mike Atherton

"The mateyness the team has displayed towards the opposition over the last month suggests the ruthless intent of last summer has been lacking"
Mike Atherton

"The number of fumbles, misfields and
grabs at thin air brought to mind some
England performances of the past...
a team full of dobbers and crap fielders?
It has been said about every England
touring team to Australia in the past
15 years. It's nice to be able to return
the compliment"
Mike Atherton

"The only one who really got up my nose
was Steve Waugh who spent the entire
series giving out verbals. A bit of a
joke really when he was the one bloke
wetting himself against the quick bowlers"
Mike Atherton

"The only positive benefit of the
injury to Flintoff may be the end of
his captaincy ambitions"
Mike Atherton

"Shane Warne turned around like a can of beans"
Mike Atherton

"Sheer pace wouldn't have worried the Indian
batsmen. Neither would ordinary bounce,
especially in England where the bowlers have
to bend their back to extract bounce. But the
mixture of both did their undoing"
*Praveen Amre on why India lost
to England in Super Eights, 2009*

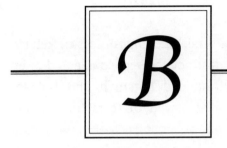

Trevor Edward Bailey
(b.1923)

Bailey was a talented English Test cricketer. A right-arm fast bowler, dependable and often dour right-handed batsman and brilliant fielder, Bailey played 61 Tests for England between 1949 and 1959. He took 132 wickets at the bowling average of 29, scored a century (134 not out) in attaining a very useful batting average of nearly 30, and took 32 catches. Perhaps his most famous achievement came at the Lord's Test in 1953 when, with England apparently facing defeat, he shared a defensive fifth wicket stand with Willie Watson, defying the Australian bowlers for over four hours to earn a draw. England went on to regain The Ashes.

~

"I don't think he expected it, and that's what caught him unawares"
Trevor Bailey

"On the first day, Logie decided to chance his arm and it came off"
Trevor Bailey

"The first time you face up to a googly you're going to be in trouble if you've never faced one before"
Trevor Bailey

"Then there was that dark horse with the
golden arm, Mudassar Nazar"
Trevor Bailey

"The Port Elizabeth ground is more of a
circle than an oval, it's long and square"
Trevor Bailey

"We owe some gratitude to Gatting
and Lamb who breathed some life
into a corpse which had nearly expired"
Trevor Bailey

"... an innings of neurotic violence, of eccentric watchfulness, of brainless impetuosity and incontinent savagery. It was an extraordinary innings, a masterpiece and it secured the Ashes for England"
Simon Barnes on Kevin Pietersen's Ashes winning innings, 2005

"The traditional dress of the Australian cricketer is the baggy green cap on the head and the chip on the shoulder. Both are ritualistically assumed"
Simon Barnes

Stumped Again!

"Well, Wally, I've been watching this match
both visually and on TV..."
Ken Barrington

Richard "Richie" Benaud OBE
(b.1930)

A former Australian cricketer, and one of the greatest leg-spinners to have played Test cricket, Benaud has become one of the most recognizable and popular commentators in the game.

After retiring from playing in 1963, Benaud turned to full-time cricket journalism and commentary, dividing his time between Britain (where he worked for the BBC for many years, prior to joining Channel 4) and Australia (for Nine Network). Overall he played in or commentated on approximately 500 Test matches.

With Channel 4's loss of the rights to broadcast live Test match cricket to Sky

Sports, the 2005 Ashes series was the last that Benaud commentated on in Britain.

~

"Captaincy is 90% luck and 10% skill"
Richie Benaud

"He's usually a good puller, but he couldn't get it up that time"
Richie Benaud

"His throw went absolutely nowhere near where it was going"
Richie Benaud

"Laird has been brought in to stand in the
corner of the circle"
Richie Benaud

"The only possible result is a draw. The
alternative is a win for England"
Richie Benaud

"That slow motion replay won't show how
fast the ball was travelling"
Richie Benaud

"The kindest thing you can say about their
performance is that it was shoddy but you
can think of many stronger words to use"
Richie Benaud

"This shirt is unique, there are
only 200 of them"
Richie Benaud

"It's been a very slow and dull day, but it
hasn't been boring. It's been a good,
entertaining day's cricket"
Tony Benneworth

Henry Calthorpe Blofeld
(b.1939)

Known as "Blowers", thanks to the late Brian Johnston, Blofeld is possibly best known for his cricket commentory for BBC Radio 4, although he also commentated for ITV in the 1960s and for BSkyB from 1991 to 1994.

His cricket commentary is famous and admired for his rich and mellow voice and his particular mention of superfluous detail, such as pigeons, buses, and helicopters that happen to be passing by. He frequently makes mistakes (often not being able to identify players) and is quite often lost for words in the more exciting passages of play but this doesn't seem to matter one jot to the many loyal listeners to TMS over the world. Indeed, his popularity was highlighted in a Test against Pakistan at Headingley in 1996, when a flat overlooking the ground was draped with a huge banner proclaiming "Henry Blofeld is God".

~

"In the rear, the small diminutive figure of Shoaib Mohammed, who can't be much taller or shorter than he is"
Henry Blofeld

"I hope the umpires aren't going by the clock on the old pavilion as it's got no hands on it"
Henry Blofeld

"In Hampshire's innings, the Smith brothers scored 13 and 52 respectively"
Henry Blofeld

"Kevin Pietersen looks like a meerkat"
Ravi Bopara

"Now I've come in to the squad, the standard of football has improved"
Ravi Bopara

"Stuart Broad reminds me of a woman"
Ravi Bopara

"What do you think this is, a f***ing
tea party? No, you can't have a f***ing glass
of water. You can f***ing wait like all the
rest of us"
Allan Border to Robin Smith

"If The Poms Bat First,
Tell The Taxi To Wait"
Banner at a Test match in Sydney

"Alderman knows that he's either going to
get a wicket, or he isn't"
Steve Brenkley

Ian "Beefy", "Both" and "Guy (the Gorilla)" Botham OBE
(b.1955)

Sir Ian Terence Botham is a former England Test cricketer and Test team captain, and current cricket commentator.

Botham seems to have been single-minded from an early age... On learning that Botham wanted to be a sportsman, the careers master at his school apparently said to him, "Fine, everyone wants to play sport, but what are you really going to do?"

Good at both football and cricket, Botham opted for cricket as a career and was a genuine all-rounder with 14 centuries and 383 wickets in Test cricket. He also held a number of Test cricket records, and still holds the record for the highest number of wickets taken by an England bowler.

Somewhat controversial on and off field, and often referred to as a 'larger than life' character, Botham was the top English cricketer of the 1980s and the leading sports personality of the time. He was elected a Wisden cricketer of the year in 1978 and was voted the BBC Sports Personality of the Year in 1981. He was awarded the OBE in 1992, and knighted in 2007. He was inducted into the ICC Cricket Hall of Fame in August 2009.

Botham is President of Leukaemia Research (see www.beefy25.com).

∽

"All you Aussies are a bunch of hicks who
don't know the first thing about cricket"
Ian Botham

"Aussies are big and empty, just like
their country"
Ian Botham

"Bloody medieval most of them"
*Ian Botham on the English cricket
administration, 1995*

"Chappell was a coward. He needed
a crowd around him before he would
say anything. He was sour like milk that had
been sitting in the sun for a week"
Ian Botham

"England need to pick players who do not
have skeletons in their coffins"
Ian Botham

"He crossed the line between eccentricity
and idiocy far too often for someone who
was supposed to be running English cricket"
Ian Botham on Ted Dexter

"If I had my way I would take him to
Traitor's Gate and personally hang,
draw and quarter him"
Ian Botham on Ray Illingworth

"If you're playing against the Australians
you don't walk"
Ian Botham

"I go in planes and helicopters
because they're meant to fly.
Commentary boxes aren't"
*Ian Botham, refusing to climb into a
high-rise commentary box (for Sky)*

"Let's face it. If I can't do a better job for Sri Lanka than Ray Illingworth is doing for England then something is very wrong"
Ian Botham

"Twenty20 is like a rich slice of chocolate cake that puts the finishing touch to a meal"
Ian Botham

"After their 60 overs, the West Indies have scored 244 for 7 all out"
Frank Bough

Geoffrey Boycott
(b.1940)

A former Yorkshire and England cricketer, Boycott had a successful career from 1962 to 1986, establishing himself as one of England's finest opening batsmen. His highest Test score was 246 not out in June 1967, but he was dropped for the next match for slow scoring. He spent from 1974 to 1977 in self-imposed exile from the England team, claiming he had simply lost his appetite for Test cricket.

Later, Boycott became an often outspoken cricket commentator for both radio and television, adopting a 'tell-it-how-it-is' style delivery, and is consequently known for criticizing players. On one particular occasion, after witnessing a dropped catch, he remarked, "I reckon my mum could have caught that in her pinny."

"Hauritz doesn't look like he could bowl my mum out, then he gets our best batsman out"
Geoff Boycott

"I think England will win a Test. My concern is Australia will probably win two"
Geoff Boycott

"Michael Clarke has come down the wicket,
which he normally does with his feet"
Geoff Boycott

"He was the England cricket coach
but he always had a face like thunder.
He gave the impression he was walking
around with piles"
Geoff Boycott

"The only thing I am frightened of
is getting out"
Geoff Boycott

"And England win by a solitary 9 runs"
Frank Bough

"I've been in a few adverts but I haven't
got the body to be posing about in my
underwear like David Beckham"
Stuart Broad

"Playing against a team with
Ian Chappell as a captain turns a cricket
match into gang warfare"
Mike Brearley

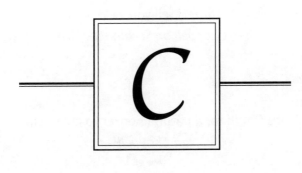

Stumped Again!

"I'd like to see him go out and bat one day
with a stump. I tell you, he'd do okay"
Greg Chappell on Sachin Tendulkar

"It's tough for a natural hooker to give it up"
Ian Chappell

"The one thing you know about Pakistan is
that you have no idea what they will do"
Ian Chappell

"The other advantage England have
got when Phil Tufnell is bowling is that
he is not fielding"
Ian Chappell

"The Test Match begins in ten minutes
– that's our time, of course"
David Coleman

"It's been hard to penetrate their batsmen"
Paul Collingwood

"Harmison likes to play every shot in the book, sometimes to the same ball"
Charles Colville

"It's been a fabulous day for England in Mumbai but not for England. Let's go back there now to celebrate with England"
Charles Colville

"It's Friday evening here. The first Test between England and India starts next Wednesday at 4 a.m., so nip upstairs now and set your alarms for that one"
Charles Colville

"Well, Pietersen wasn't even into double
figures, he'd only scored 15"
Charles Colville

"The Queens Park Oval, as its name
suggests, is absolutely round"
Tony Crozier

"Ravi Bopara makes everyone laugh
a lot, although it's mainly for always
being late or stupid"
Alastair Cook

David Gower: "Do you want Gatt
a foot wider?"
Chris Cowdrey: "No. He'd burst"

"England have their noses in front, not
only actually but metaphorically too"
Tony Crozier

Interviewer: "Darryl, who are your
favourite actors?"
Darryl Cullinan: "Dustin Hoffman and
some Aussie bowlers in the act of
appealing"

"Go and deflate yourself, you balloon"
Daryll Cullinan to Shane Warne

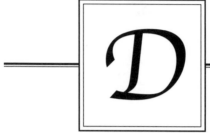

"England were beaten in the sense
that they lost"
Dickie Davis

"That's a remarkable catch by Yardley,
especially as the ball quite literally rolled
along the ground towards him"
Mike Denness

"If you are going to lose, you might
as well lose good and proper and try to
sneak a win"
Ted Dexter

"I have on occasion taken a quite
reasonable dislike to the Australians"
Ted Dexter

"I think we are all slightly down in the
dumps after another loss. We may be
in the wrong sign... Venus
may be in the wrong juxtaposition
with somewhere else"
Ted Dexter

"Once again our cricketers have flattered
to deceive in Australia"
Ted Dexter

"Cricket is a very cruel game. The moment
you relax is when you are in trouble"
Mahendra Singh Dhoni

"It's not the first time I have been booed.
When we lost in 2007 World Cup, *mera
antim sanskar* [last rites] was also done.
But I don't feel bad. It shows the
expectation levels of fans"
*Mahendra Singh Dhoni on being booed by
the fans during the presentation ceremony
after the match against England, June 2009*

"There is a widely held and quite erroneous
belief that cricket is just another game"
HRH the Duke of Edinburgh

"It's difficult to be more laid back
than David Gower without being
actually comatose"
Frances Edmonds

"Monty Panesar needs to pull
his length back"
John Emburey

Stumped Again!

"To be honest, the f*cking f*cker is
f*cking f*cked!"
*John Emburey, when asked about his injury
in 1997*

"Derek Randall bats like an octopus
with piles"
Matthew Engel

"If Gower hadn't caught that, it would
have decapitated his hand"
Farokh Engineer

"Sunny, don't get out first ball. It's a long
way back to the pavilion"
Farokh Engineer,
who was dismissed first ball

"Waugh! What is he good for?
Absolutely nothing!"
England fans' song
during the 1993 Ashes series

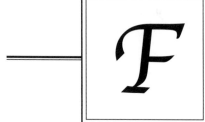

Andrew "Freddie" Flintoff MBE
(b.1977)

Nicknamed "Freddie" and "Fred" (owing to the similarity between his surname and that of Fred Flintstone, and the issues he had with his weight when he first emerged onto the scene).

An English cricketer, after his debut in 1998, Flintoff become an integral player for England, and both captained and vice-captained the team. He also played for Lancashire County Cricket Club, and the Indian Premier League team Chennai Super Kings.

In July 2009 Flintoff announced his retirement from Test cricket at the conclusion of the 2009 Ashes series, but made himself available for future commitments in One Day International and Twenty20 International matches.

A fast bowler, batsman and slip fielder, Flintoff suffered regular injuries throughout his international career, often due to his heavy frame and bowling action. However, according to the ICC rankings, he was consistently rated amongst the top international all-rounders in both ODI and Test cricket.

Flintoff was crowned BBC Sports Personality of the Year in 2005 (the first cricketer since Ian Botham in 1981). He was appointed an MBE in the New Year's Honours List for 2006 and the same year was presented with the Freedom of the City award for Preston, Lancashire.

∼

"After the Ashes victory, I got a lift back
to the hotel with Steve Harmison but
I was so carried away with drink and
emotion, I spoke Egyptian"
Andrew Flintoff

"Getting to know Botham as a person
has helped because I'm no longer in awe of
him as much as I was when I started"
Andrew Flintoff

"I'm completely different from Pietersen.
He would turn up to the opening of an
envelope"
Andrew Flintoff

"I'm looking forward to spending more time
watching *Coronation Street*"
Andrew Flintoff

"I'm not sure if I'm looking forward to facing
Brett Lee again. He bowls at 95 mph so
enjoyment is not the word I would use"
Andrew Flintoff

"I'm ugly, I'm overweight, but I'm happy"
Andrew Flintoff

"I was just here for the food!"
*Andrew Flintoff, after being announced joint
ICC player of the year 2005*

"I remember the first time I walked into
the Lancashire dressing-room, when
I was 16... All these guys, Atherton,
Fairbrother, Akram... you just drop your
shopping, you don't know where to put
yourself. With Botham, I could barely pick
my shopping up"
*Andrew Flintoff on the first time
he met Ian Botham*

"Not bad for a fat lad"
*Andrew Flintoff, on accepting
a man of the match award*

"People will be surprised by this, but I'm
actually very scared of the dark"
Andrew Flintoff

"There was a tear in my eye. Then I saw a TV
camera and I thought, 'Nobody is going to
see me crying'. So I nipped into the toilet
and gave myself a minute to pull myself
together – then got on with celebrating"
*Andrew Flintoff, after playing
his final Test match*

"There are two kinds of batsmen
in the world. One: Sachin Tendulkar.
Two: all the others"
Andy Flower

"I'm left-handed in nearly everything
I do – golf, cricket, everything except
kicking a ball"
Daniel Flynn

G

"Glenn McGrath joins Craig McDermott and
Paul Reiffel in a three-ponged prace attack"
Tim Gavel

Interviewer to Mike Gatting: "Do you
feel that the selectors and yourself have
been vindicated by the result?"
Mike Gatting: "I don't think the press
are vindictive. They can write what
they want"

"I'm not crazy but I talk to myself.
And sometimes I answer back"
Chris Gayle

"It was a mixture of bad bowling, good
shots and arse"
*Jason Gillespie, describing his own
Ashes performance*

"If it had been a cheese roll, it would
never have got past him"
Graham Gooch

"A fart competing with thunder"
*Graham Gooch on England's chances in
Australia in 1990-91*

"The Sri Lankan team have lost
their heads – literally"
Gamine Goonasena

"Illy [Ray Illingworth] had the
man-management skills of Basil Fawlty"
Darren Gough

"It's hard work making batting
look effortless"
David Gower

"Yes, he's a very good cricketer but it's a pity
he's not a better batter or bowler"
Tom Graveney

Anthony "Tony" William Greig
(b.1946)

Although born in South Africa, Greig qualified to play for England by virtue of his Scottish father and became captain of the national side from 1975 to 1977.

Sometimes a controversial figure, Greig helped Kerry Packer start World Series Cricket by signing up not only many of his English colleagues but also West Indian and Pakistani cricketers; a daring act that cost him the captaincy of England. Packer later offered Greig a 'job for life' as a commentator during Nine's cricket coverage.

Today, Greig lives in Australia and continues his commentary role. He has been criticized for his bias against the Australian team and for his occasional out-of-context comments. Greig also has commentated for Channel 4 in the UK.

~

"David Lloyd is speaking to his slippers"
Tony Greig

"Clearly the West Indies are going to play their normal game, which is what they normally do"
Tony Greig

"Marshall's bowling with his head"
Tony Greig

"Geoff Boycott has the uncanny knack of
being where fast bowlers aren't"
Tony Greig

"In the back of Hughes' mind must
be the thought that he will dance down
the piss and mitch one"
Tony Greig

"The Aussies try to present a tough
guy image, but this present generation
are a bunch of cissies"
Tony Greig

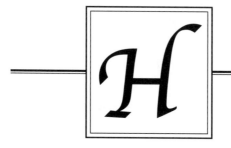

"I used to think cricket was fun.
Then I saw Tendulkar bat"
Chris Hansen

"Shane Warne's idea of a balanced diet
is a cheeseburger in each hand"
Ian Healy

"These last five weeks have passed by
at the drop of a pin"
Rachel Heyhoe-Flint

"Cricket needs brightening up a bit. My solution is to let the players drink at the beginning of the game, not after. It always works in our picnic matches"
Paul Hogan

"In most cricketing dismissals there's usually a human element involved"
Michael Holding

"The one thing Australian batsmen don't like is those dibbly dobbers"
Michael Holding

"I'll bowl you a fucking piano, you Pommie
poof! Let's see if you can play that!"
Merv Hughes to Michael Atherton,
1989 Ashes

"Other than his mistakes, he hasn't
put a foot wrong"
Simon Hughes

"The great thing about Stuart Broad is that
his length probes relentlessly"
Simon Hughes

"Devon Smith looks like the sort of guy you
can imagine pumping himself"
Nasser Hussain

"Jimmy Andersen will have to get his
length right when he faces Butt"
Nasser Hussain

"Ponting will be thinking, we dished up filth"
Nasser Hussain

"Stuart Broad is putting it in the batsman's slot"
Nasser Hussain

"He's got his hands up in the middle
of his arms"
Nasser Hussain

"Michael Clarke desperately wants a
couple of extra inches"
Nasser Hussain

"There's a concern for cricket because
the goal posts are moving"
Nasser Hussain

1

"As harrowing occupations go, there
can't be much to choose between the
Australian cricket captaincy
and social work on Skid Row"
Doug Ibbotson

"He stood on tiptoe, on the back foot,
and drove the ball on the off. I don't quite
know how you'd describe that shot"
Ray Illingworth

"That black cloud is coming from the
direction the wind is blowing, now the wind
is coming from where the black cloud is"
Ray Illingworth

Stumped Again!

"The statistics suggest that Mike Brearley is
one of the great England captains. The
luckiest would be nearer the truth"
Ray Illingworth

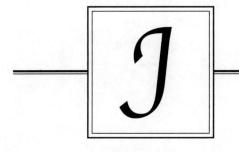

"Pollock is such a good bowler
it hasn't even taken him a single delivery
to get it on the spot"
Robin Jackman

"That Glenn McGrath... what a bastard!"
Mick Jagger

"All Australians are an uneducated
and unruly mob"
*Douglas Jardine to Australian wicket keeper
Stork Hendry during the infamous
1932-1933 Bodyline series*

"Well bowled, Harold!"
Douglas Jardine, after Larwood felled
Woodfull with a ball in the chest

"England have spun, swung and swatted
their way to an incredible triumph"
Boris Johnson on England
winning the Ashes 2009

Brian Alexander Johnston
(1912-1994)

Known fondly as "Johnners", Johnston was a cricket commentator for the BBC from 1946 until his death. He began his cricket commentating career at Lord's for BBC Television in June 1946 at the England v. India Test match.

Johnston was responsible for a number of the BBC's Test Match Special team's traditions, including giving nicknames to fellow commentators – Jonathan Agnew is still known as "Aggers", Henry Blofeld as "Blowers" and Bill Frindall as "the Bearded Wonder"!

Johnston's informal and humorous style was very popular. When he died, the Daily Telegraph described him as "the greatest natural broadcaster of them all", and John Major remarked that "summers will never be the same".

Johnston's memorial service was held at a crowded Westminster Abbey in May, 1994. The following year the Brian Johnston Memorial Trust was established, to promote cricket in schools and youth clubs, and to help young cricketers in need of financial support.

~

Stumped Again!

"And I can see a strong wind blowing
the sun towards us"
Brian Johnston

"And now it's over to Rex Alston
for some balls"
Brian Johnston

"And that's Dickie Bird standing there with
his neck between his shoulders"
Brian Johnston

"Butcher plays this off the black foot"
Brian Johnston

"Ray Illingworth has just
relieved himself at the pavilion end"
Brian Johnston

"This bowler's like my dog: three short
legs and balls that swing each way"
Brian Johnston

Stumped Again!

"I don't think I've ever seen anything quite like that before, and it's the second time it's happened today"
Brian Johnston

"Jim is such a snob that he won't travel in the same car as his chauffeur"
Brian Johnston

"Welcome to Worcester where you've just missed seeing Barry Richards hitting one of Basil D'Oliveira's balls clean out of the ground"
Brian Johnston

"He's twisted his ankle and is in excruciating
pain. It's especially bad as he's here on his
honeymoon. Still, he'll probably be all right
tomorrow if he sticks it up tonight"
Brian Johnston

"And a sedentary seagull flies by"
Brian Johnston

"England have only three major problems.
They can't bat, they can't bowl and they
can't field"
Martin Johnson

"The mincing run-up resembles
someone in high heels and a panty girdle
chasing after a bus"
Martin Johnson on Merv Hughes

"It's interesting to see each other's balls.
Mine's, one side is a little bit rougher than
Ben Hilfenhaus"
Mitchell Johnson

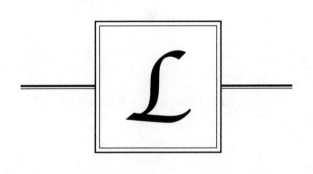

"And Ian Greig's on eight, including two fours"
Jim Laker

"An interesting morning, full of interest"
Jim Laker

"It's a unique occasion, really – a repeat of
Melbourne 1977"
Jim Laker

"The aim of English test cricket is, in fact,
mainly to beat Australia"
Jim Laker

"A cricket tour in Australia would be
the most delightful period in one's life,
if one was deaf"
Harold Larwood

"The selectors are full of shit"
Chris Lewis on not being picked in 1998

"Kapil Dev seems to have a
preconceived idea in his head, but he
doesn't seem to know what it is"
Tony Lewis

"For any budding cricketers listening,
do you have any superstitious routines
before an innings, like putting one pad on
first and then the other?"
Tony Lewis

"He fell in love with himself at a very young
age and has remained faithful ever since"
Dennis Lillee on Geoff Boycott

"Hell, Gatt, move out of the way,
I can't see the stumps"
Dennis Lillee

"If I've to bowl to Sachin, I'll bowl with my
helmet on. He hits the ball so hard"
Dennis Lillee

"300 for 4. A couple more wickets
and it'll be 300 for 6"
David Lloyd

"Aussie 12th man Ronald McDonald
brought on a triple burger with relish.
But England need a large scotch!"
David Lloyd

"Graeme Smith showed us how big
he can get"
David Lloyd

"He's a very dangerous bowler,
innocuous if you like"
David Lloyd

"Ricky Ponting looks like how
I would imagine Jimmy Krankie
would've turned out with the aid
of human growth hormones"
Gabby Logan

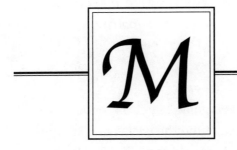

Stumped Again!

"So how's your wife, and my kids?"
Rod Marsh's aside to Ian Botham
during a match

"Are you going to get out or do I have
to come round the wicket and kill you?"
Malcolm Marshall to David Boon

"You convicts are all the same"
Malcolm Marshall to Steve Waugh after
he refused to walk

"It's his second finger, technically his third"
Christopher Martin-Jenkins

"Say, when do they begin?"
*Groucho Marx, watching a cricket match
at Lord's*

"If you go in with two fast bowlers
and one breaks down, you're left two short"
Bob Massie

Stumped Again!

"Chappell just stood on his feet and
smashed it to the boundary"
Jim Maxwell

"The sight of Bright holds no fright
for Wright"
Jim Maxwell

"You've got to bat on this in a minute,
Tufnell. Hospital food suit you?"
Craig McDermott

"This game will be over any time from now"
Alan McGilvray

"It's amazing! When you actually watch a
ball you can actually see it a lot better"
Glenn McGrath

"So that's 57 runs needed by Hampshire
in 11 overs and it doesn't need a calculator
to tell you that the run rate is 5.1818"
Norman de Mesquita

"He only came unstuck against the ball
that bowled him"
Simon Metcalf

"Are you aware, sir, that the last time I saw
anything like that on a top lip, the whole
herd had to be destroyed?"
Eric Morecambe to Dennis Lillee

"A Yorkshire team without a left-arm
slow bowler would be like an army
without its general, a jockey without
a horse, a fish without chips"
Don Mosey

"Boycott, somewhat a creature of habit,
likes exactly the sort of food
he himself prefers"
Don Mosey

"He'll certainly want to start
by getting off the mark"
Don Mosey

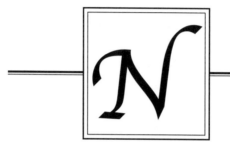

"It's a funny kind of month, October.
For the really keen cricket fan,
it's when you realize
that your wife left you in May"
Denis Norden

"Cunnis – that's a funny name, neither one
thing or the other"
New Zealand commentator

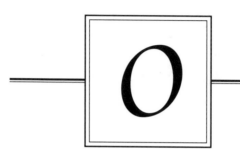

Mark Waugh: "F*ck me, look who it is. Mate, what are you doing out here? There's no way you're good enough to play for England!"
James Ormond: "Maybe not, but at least I'm the best player in my family"

"I think I fancy Graham Onions more than Freddie [Flintoff] now. I've heard he goes for days"
Lily Allen on her twitter feed, August 2009

"She has obviously not seen me in real life... it would be a pleasure to meet her"
Graham Onions on a chance to meet Lily Allen, August 2009

P

Kevin Pietersen MBE
(b.1980)

Pietersen is a cricketer, an attacking right-handed batsman and occasional off-spin bowler who plays for England and Hampshire. He is widely portrayed in the media as having a self-assured personality, and Geoff Boycott once described him as being "cocky and confident". He is noted for his unusual haircuts, with his peroxide-blond streak of hair along the middle of his head being described as a "skunk" (or sometimes even "dead skunk") look.

≈

"For some strange reason, my hands
have gone outside my eyes"
Kevin Pietersen

"I'm not very good at Twenty20 cricket,
am I? The more you play T20 cricket the
better you become and I haven't played
a lot of it, and I'm not very good at it"
Kevin Pietersen

"It's definitely not a silly game anymore.
You see the money involved and the cricket
as well and in the few weeks we could win
a World Cup"
Kevin Pietersen on Twenty20 cricket

"I've dropped six catches and nobody's given me a beer"
Kevin Pietersen

"He's a massive, massive, big, fat, ugly bear. I'm allowed to say that because he and I always compare each other's skin folds in the dressing room"
Kevin Pietersen on Ravi Bopara

"It's only a matter of time before the end of this innings"
Michael Peschardt

"I tend to think that cricket is the greatest
thing that God ever created on earth –
certainly greater than sex, although sex
isn't too bad either"
Harold Pinter

"After I've played a shot, I switch off, maybe
think about sex and get ready to go again"
Ricky Ponting

"If we have an early exit, we'll have two
weeks in Leicester. That won't be good
for anybody"
Ricky Ponting

"I still rank England second"
Ricky Ponting

"There's a tendency for balls to swing
around here and hopefully we can
take a few early wickets"
Ricky Ponting

"It was close for Zaheer, Lawson
threw his hands in the air and Marsh
threw his head in the air"
Jack Potter

Stumped Again!

"Shane Warne is thicker than a complete
set of Wisden yearbooks"
Matt Price

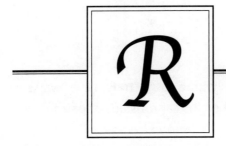

"Sachin is cricket's God"
Barry Richards

"The only time an Australian ever walks
is when his car runs out of petrol"
Barry Richards

"He's 99.5 percent perfect"
Viv Richards on Sachin Tendulkar

"Man, it don't matter where you come
in to bat, the score is still zero"
Viv Richards

"One-day cricket is like fast food.
No one wants to cook"
Viv Richards

"Helmets are unfair to bowlers"
Viv Richards

Greg Thomas was bowling to Viv Richards in
a county game. Viv missed a superb
outswinger and Thomas said, "It's red,
round and weighs about 5 ounces."
With the next ball Richards hit Thomas
out of the ground and replied,
"Greg, you know what it looks like.
Go ahead and find it!"

"William Gallas is the worst skipper
since Heather Mills"
James Richardson

"Border is a walnut: hard to crack and
without much to please the eye"
Peter Roebuck

"An ordinary bloke trying to make good
without ever losing the air of a fellow
with a hangover"
Peter Roebuck on Merv Hughes

S

Stumped Again!

"I don't know what these fellows
are doing, but whatever they're doing,
they sure are doing it well"
*Pete Sampras on watching Lara and
Ambrose at Lord's*

"With his soft white hands he just
tossed it off"
Bobby Simpson

"Merv is a funny guy, though
he would sledge his own mother if he
thought it would help the cause"
Gladstone Small

"You can have violence in cricket
like you would see in a boxing ring"
Alan Stanford

"Take a good look at this arse of mine,
you'll see plenty of it this summer"
David Steele to Rodney Marsh

"I get asked, 'What's better, hitting a six
or having sex?' I don't hit that many sixes. If
I had to wait that long between stints in the
sack, my life wouldn't be too great"
Andrew Strauss

"Cricket's only a game and there are far more serious things in the world like Susan Boyle or Katie and Peter"
Graeme Swann

"I didn't know what to do when we won the Ashes. Thank God I didn't slide on my knees like a cheap medallion footballer"
Graeme Swann

"I forgot to pack enough undies, so I fashioned some briefs from a flowery lampshade and two Mars bar wrappers. Very D&G"
Graeme Swann

"I never thought a game of cricket could
make me so happy, because cricket's
basically rubbish"
Graeme Swann

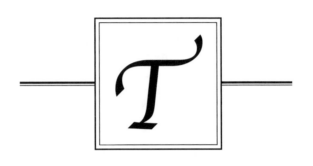

Frederick Sewards Trueman OBE
(1931-2006)

A Yorkshire and England cricketer, Trueman was regarded as one of the greatest fast bowlers in history. He was the first man to take 300 Test wickets. Known as "Fiery Fred", Trueman occasionally taunted batsmen with his Yorkshire humour and the icy glare that went with his aggressive nature.

Trueman became a popular and rather outspoken radio commentator. Famous for his dislike of many aspects of the modern game, especially one-day cricket, Trueman was criticized by some, such as Ian Botham, for being unduly negative about modern players and for making too much of cricket "in my day".

Trueman was an expert commentator for the BBC's Test Match Special, and his catchphrase "I don't know what's going off out there," summed up his dismay that modern cricketers lacked his knowledge of tactics.

He was made an OBE in 1989. After Brian Johnston, a colleague on TMS, had bestowed on him the nickname "Sir Frederick", there were those who thought he had really been knighted.

"Anyone foolish enough to predict the outcome of this match is a fool"
Fred Trueman

"A Test match without Ian Botham is like
a horror film without Boris Karloff"
Fred Trueman

"If Boycott played cricket the way he talked, he
would have had people queuing up to get into
the ground instead of queuing up to leave"
Fred Trueman

"I'd throw them off the top of the pavilion.
Mind you, I'm a fair man, I'd give them a 50-
50 chance. I'd have Keith Fletcher
underneath trying to catch them"
*Fred Trueman on the saboteurs who dug up
the Headingley Test wicket, 1975*

"That was a tremendous six. The ball was still in the air as it went over the boundary"
Fred Trueman

"That's what cricket is all about, two batsmen pitting their wits against one another"
Fred Trueman

"There's only one head bigger than Tony Greig's and that's Birkenhead"
Fred Trueman

"Unless something happens that we can't
predict, I don't think a lot will happen"
Fred Trueman

"It was a good tour to break my teeth in"
Bernard Thomas

"You cannot smoke twenty a day and
bowl fast"
Phil Tufnell

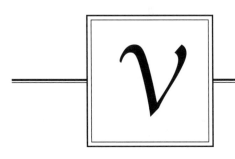

"If we don't beat you we'll knock your
bloody heads off"
Bill Voce

"Tufnell! Can I borrow your brain?
I'm building an idiot"
*Voice from the crowd during the
Newcastle Test match*

"Don't give the bastard a drink.
Let him die of thirst"
*Voice from the crowd while Jardine was
batting during the Bodyline series*

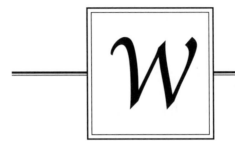

"It is important for Pakistan to take wickets
if they are going to make big inroads into
this Australian batting line-up"
Max Walker

"He's got perfect control of the ball, right up
to the moment where he lets it go"
Peter Walker

"The England women's cricket team are
such an outstanding crack unit"
Ian Ward, Sky Sports

Shane "Warney" Warne
(b.1969)

Shane Keith Warne, nicknamed "Warney", "Warnie" and "Hollywood".

Warne is a former Australian international cricketer widely regarded as one of the greatest leg spin bowlers in the history of the game.

He also played Australian domestic cricket for his home state of Victoria, and English domestic cricket for Hampshire. He was captain of Hampshire for three seasons, from 2005 to 2007.

A popular and controversial figure, Warne retired from international cricket in January 2007, at the end of Australia's 5-0 Ashes series victory over England.

Following his retirement from international cricket, Warne played a full season at Hampshire in 2007 and in March 2008 he announced his retirement from playing first-class cricket in order to be able to spend more time pursuing interests outside of the game.

Warne was named Wisden Cricketer of the Year in 1994, One-Day International Player of the Year in 2000, was selected as one of five Wisden cricketers of the century in 2000, named winner of the BBC Sports Personality of the Year Overseas Personality in 2005, and named Test Player of the Year in 2006.

~

"Gamesmanship, banter, trash talk, sledging... whatever you call it, has been part of cricket for a long time. We will play hard to win and anybody who plays us will be tested both physically and mentally. If they aren't up to it, we'll win easily"

Shane Warne

"I am Australian, as simple as that, and I always will be. I'm not going to be Adolf Warne or anything like that"

Shane Warne

"When the groundsman puts in those three stumps, that gives you a clue where to bowl"
Shane Warne

"KP's weird. He'll be in bed thinking of things no-one else ever has!"
Shane Warne

"I'll be going to bed having nightmares of Sachin just running down the wicket and belting me back over the head for six. He was unstoppable. I don't think anyone, apart from Don Bradman, is in the same class as Sachin Tendulkar. He is just an amazing player"
Shane Warne

"I always thought Ian Bell looked like Chuck
Sherman in *American Pie*. I said to him,
'What are you looking at, Shermanator?'
Bell replied, 'I've been called worse.'
'No mate,' I said, 'You know you haven't'"
Shane Warne

"The only way I'd ever consider
becoming England cricket coach is
through an offer so financially
outrageous it'd be impossible to refuse"
Shane Warne

"They remind me a bit of Laurel and Hardy,
in that they are different characters who
complement each other nicely"
Shane Warne on Flintoff and Strauss

"I used to put on weight easily. I remember
my dad picked me up at the airport and
thought I was a fat bastard he didn't know"
Shane Warne

Interviewer: "What's your favourite animal?"
Steve Waugh: "Merv Hughes"

"And we have just heard, although this is not the latest score from Bournemouth, that Hampshire have beaten Nottinghamshire by nine wickets"
Peter West

"Pietersen's just stroked Vettori through the covers"
Arlo White

"I never play cricket. It requires one to assume such indecent postures"
Oscar Wilde

"Cricket is baseball on valium"
Robin Williams

"The Aussie all-rounder Andrew McDonald
is more like Ronald McDonald"
Bob Willis

"Peter Siddle's heavy balls made life difficult"
Bob Willis

"Vengsarkar taking a simple catch at square
leg, the ball literally dropping down his throat"
Bob Willis

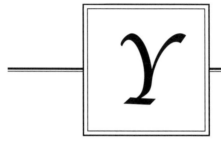

"Bowl the bastard a grand piano and see if
he can play that instead!"
Yabba

"Don't swat those flies, Jardine, they're the
only friends here you've got!"
Yabba

"Those are the only balls you've touched all
day!"
*Yabba, to an English batsman adjusting his
box in between overs*

STUMPED!

The world's funniest cricket quotes

Charlie Croker

978-1-906051-02-0

OWN GOALS!

The world's funniest football quotes

978-1-906051-42-6

www.crombiejardine.com